This Rising Moon Book Belongs to:

Over in the

Garden

Over in the Garden

by Jennifer Ward

illustrated by Kenneth J. Spengler

rising moon

www.northlandpub.com

The author would like to give special thanks to Dr. Elizabeth A. Bernays, Regents' Professor
Emeritus and Joint Professor in Ecology and Evolutionary Biology, University of Arizona,
School of Agriculture, Department of Entomology. Thank you for opening your home to
me and sharing your time and wealth of knowledge.

Composed in the United States of America

The illustrations were rendered in gouache on watercolor paper.
The text type was set in Poppl-Laudito, display type was set in Fontesque Bold.
Edited by Aimee Jackson, Designed by Chantelle Call, Production by Donna Boyd.

FIRST IMPRESSION
ISBN 0-87358-793-6

03   04   05   5   4   3   2

Library of congress Cataloging-in-Publication Data
Ward, Jennifer, 1963-
Over in the garden / by Jennifer Ward; illustrated by Kenneth J. Spengler.
p. cm
Summary: Over in the garden, mother insects and their children enjoy various activities
from morning sun to evening moon.

[1. Insects--Fiction. 2. Counting. 3. Stories in rhyme.] I. Spengler, Kenneth. II. title.

PZ8.3.W2135 Ov 2001
[E]--dc21   2001019772

For Rich.
— J.W.

To all those little creatures
that fill my life with joy and fear.
— K.S.

Hey, kids!
Look for
the number
hidden on
each page!

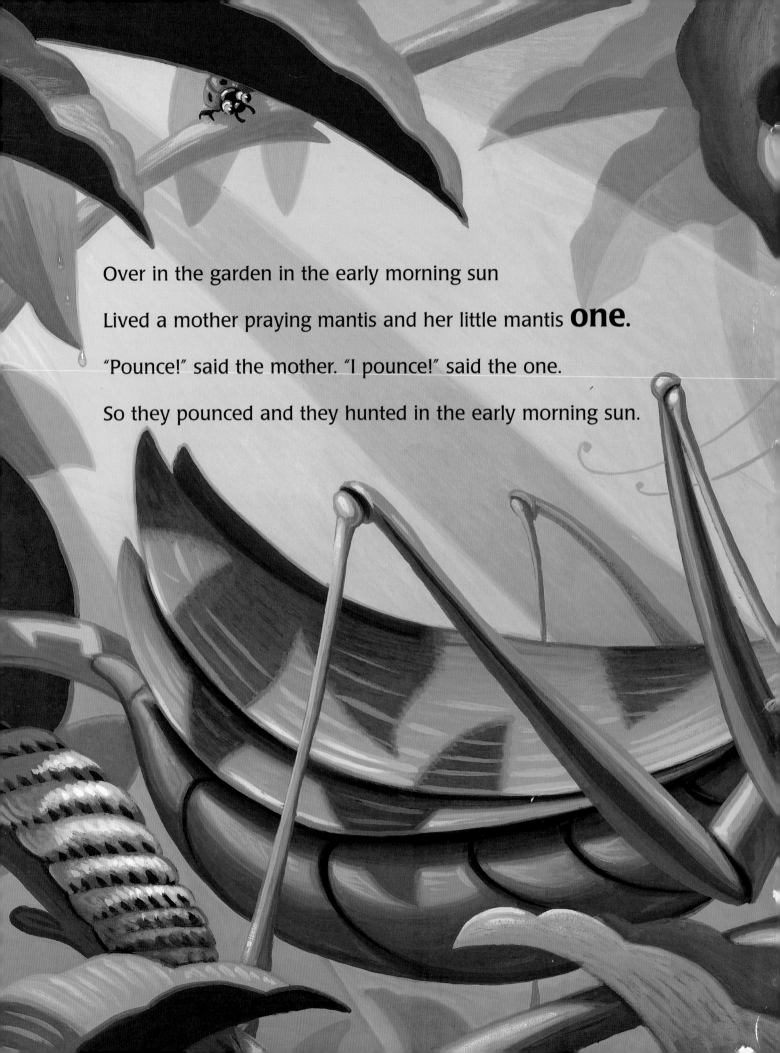

Over in the garden in the early morning sun

Lived a mother praying mantis and her little mantis **one**.

"Pounce!" said the mother. "I pounce!" said the one.

So they pounced and they hunted in the early morning sun.

Over in the garden where the sunflowers grew

Lived a mother ladybug and her little beetles **two**.

"Crawl!" said the mother. "We crawl!" said the two.

So they crawled over petals where the sunflowers grew.

Over in the garden near the old shady tree

Lived a mother dragonfly and her little dragons **three**.

"Zip!" said the mother. "We zip!" said the three.

So they zipped and they zoomed near the old shady tree.

Over in the garden on the damp, earthy floor

Lived a quiet mother snail and her baby snails **four**.

"Slither!" said the mother. "We slither!" said the four.

So they slithered and they slid on the damp, earthy floor.

Over in the garden where the apple blossoms thrive

Lived a colony of bees and their little bees **five**.

"Buzz!" said the workers. "We buzz!" said the five.

So they buzzed and they flew where the apple blossoms thrive.

Over in the garden where the vines and berries mix

Lived a little mother spider and her baby spiders **six**.

"Jump!" said the mother. "We jump!" said the six.

So they jumped through the garden where the vines and berries mix.

Over in the garden where the flowers grow toward heaven

Lived a mother butterfly and her caterpillars **seven**.

"Nibble!" said the mother. "We nibble!" said the seven.

So they nibbled and they climbed

where the flowers grow

toward heaven.

Over in the garden by the old wooden gate

Lived a mother roly-poly and her little babies **eight**.

"Roll!" said the mother. "We roll!" said the eight.

So they rolled and they curled by the old wooden gate.

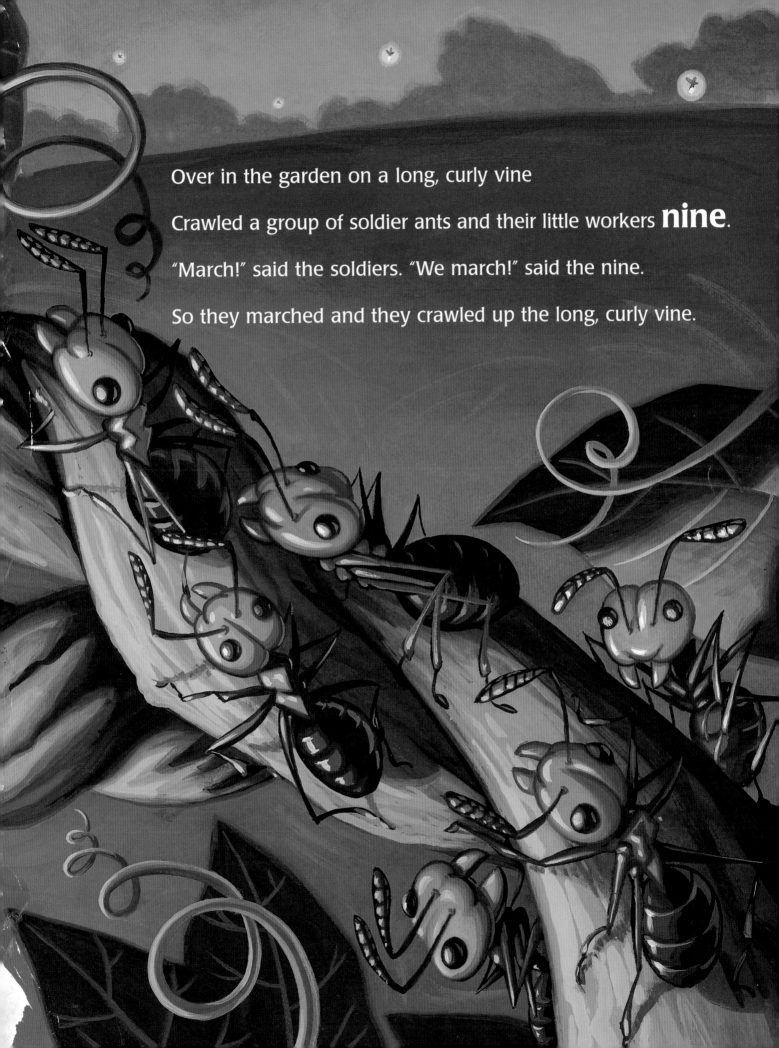

Over in the garden on a long, curly vine

Crawled a group of soldier ants and their little workers **nine**.

"March!" said the soldiers. "We march!" said the nine.

So they marched and they crawled up the long, curly vine.

Over in the garden where the moon shines again

Lived a mother firefly and her little beetles **ten**.

"Glow!" said the mother. "We glow!" said the ten.

So they glowed and they flashed where the moon shines again.

Fun Facts

Ant—There are many different types of ants and all of them are social insects. This means they live within a colony and all of the ants in the colony work together to provide food and shelter for the young. An ant colony has a queen. She is the mother ant and lays all the eggs. The queen is taken care of by the worker ants, who gather food, take care of the larvae, and keep the nest clean. Some types of ants have very large worker ants, called soldiers. Ant colonies come in different sizes, from just a dozen ants in a colony to several million!

Arachnid—Arachnids have four pairs of walking legs, for a total of eight legs. They include spiders, scorpions and mites. Can you find the arachnid in this story?

Arthropod—These are animals that have a hard, protective body case and jointed legs. Arthropods include insects, arachnids, crustaceans, centipedes, and millipedes. Arthropods make up the largest group of animals found on earth!

Bee—There are many species of bees. Some live socially while others live alone. The bees in this story live socially within a colony. They have a queen and many worker bees who take care of the queen and the larvae.

Beetle—Beetles are insects that have a pair of hard wing cases. The hard wing case is an outer covering that protects their other pair of wings, called flight wings. Flight wings are folded underneath the hard wing cases when they are not being used. Beetles go through a metamorphosis before becoming an adult. From the beetle egg comes a larva. Then the larva turns into a pupa which will then turn into an adult. The beetles in this story are the ladybug and the firefly.

Bug–A lot of people use the word "bug" when talking about all arthropods or insects, but true bugs are only those that have mouth parts that can pierce and suck! Most true bugs suck juices and saps from plants. There are no true bugs in this story.

Butterfly–This is an insect that goes through a metamorphosis during its life. First, it begins its life as an egg. The egg then hatches into a caterpillar. The caterpillar then changes into a pupa, which is also sometimes called a chrysalis. From the pupa comes a butterfly. All butterflies have four wings which are covered with tiny and often colorful scales. Butterflies are active during the day and can often be seen flying through gardens in search of flowers to sip nectar from.

Caterpillar–Caterpillars come from butterfly or moth eggs. Caterpillars spend their time eating and eating and growing and growing. When a caterpillar is fully grown, it changes into a pupa. In time, a butterfly or moth will emerge from the pupa.

Dragonfly–These insects have four large, clear wings and hunt other insects while flying through the air. They lay their eggs in water and when the eggs hatch, the babies continue to live in the water and are called nymphs. In time, the nymphs crawl out of the water and molt into winged, adult dragonflies.

Firefly–This is a beetle that produces a flashing light in its abdomen. The male and female fireflies use the light to find each other at night.

Insect–Insects have three main body parts; a head, a thorax, and an abdomen. Insects are invertebrates, which means they do not have a backbone. It is estimated that 10 quintillion–10,000,000,000,000,000,000 insects are alive on earth at any time!

Ladybug—Ladybugs are beetles that are usually brightly colored. The bright colors help to warn off predators that might want to eat the ladybug. Ladybugs love to eat aphids. Aphids are true bugs that can damage gardens by sucking out plant juices. Therefore, many people love to find ladybugs living in their gardens!

Larva—This is a life stage between egg and pupa for insects that go through a metamorphosis. The larva will often look completely different from the adult it will turn into.

Metamorphosis—This is the change that occurs from larva to adult.

Nymph—A nymphs is a baby insect that does not go through a complete metamorphosis. The nymph resembles the adult but does not have wings. The dragonflies and the praying mantis are nymphs before growing into adults.

Praying Mantis—The praying mantis is an insect that is predatory. This means that it hunts other insects. It has very large eyes that help it to see its prey. Often, the praying mantis will sit very still and wait for its prey to come along. Then, in a flash, the praying mantis will pounce and the unsuspecting prey becomes a meal.

 **Roly-poly**—Also known as a wood louse, sow bug, or pill bug, this animal is a crustacean and is related to crabs and lobsters. It has a segmented body and seven pairs of legs. It may curl up into a ball for protection.

Over in the Garden

O - ver in the gar - den in the ear - ly mor-ning

sun Lived a mo-ther pray-ing man-tis and her

lit - tle man - tis one. "Pounce!" said the mo-ther. "I

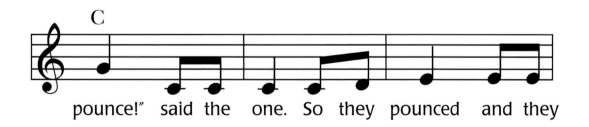

pounce!" said the one. So they pounced and they

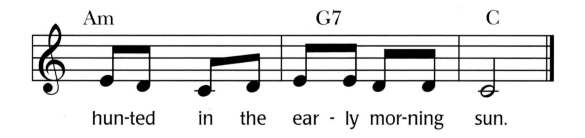

hun-ted in the ear - ly mor-ning sun.

Jennifer Ward has been writing stories for as long as she can remember. She loves to use her earliest stories, some written as young as age six, along with her published titles, to inspire children of all ages with their own writing. *Over in the Garden* is the third companion title following *Somewhere in the Ocean*, a 2000 Parents Choice Award Winner, and *Way Out in the Desert*, a 2000 Arizona Young Readers' Award nominee, all from Rising Moon.

Kenneth J. Spengler began his career as an illustrator shortly after he graduated from Tyler School of Art with a B. F. A. His work can be found on anything from posters to billboards, and from mystery covers to children's books such as *Way Out in the Desert* and *A Campfire for Cowboy Billy,* both from Rising Moon.